The Personal Side

of Policing

By

Dr. Alfred S. Titus, Jr.

The Personal Side of Policing

ISBN-13: 978-0-692-11875-7 (paperback)

DEDICATION

This book is dedicated to the eager youth to whom I
have had the pleasure of lecturing throughout my career,
both on the streets and in the classroom.

May each of you benefit from this compilation of
information and achieve the success you desire in the
field of law enforcement.

Remember, anything in life is what you make it!

THE WORLD IS YOURS!

The Personal Side of Policing

By Dr. Alfred S. Titus, Jr.

Chapters

Foreword

We live in a world where society believes they are fully informed about policing. Society feels they know what should be done, why it should be done, and how it should be done. The many misconceptions in policing are derived from television, movies, and emotionally charged participation in the process. Policing is actually a science with intricate parts that work in conjunction with each other to maintain order in our society. The perceptions of late are that of a completely different thing.

There is no doubt that the science of policing has not been perfected, however every effort is being made to create a science with few flaws. There are errors made, controversial decisions made, and failures to recognize issues efficiently at times. These are issues that exist in every part of our lives. To expect policing to be different is absurd. My hope is that this book will provide some insight into what an officer or agent deals with. It is just a small look at all that the obligation and responsibility undertaken entails. With this small view of the inside, I hope some understanding can be gained.

This book is written for everyone interested in a career in law enforcement, those already in law enforcement, and those who are curious about gaining insight about the field. It is written from my perspective based on my 23-year law enforcement career and experiences in the New York City Police Department (NYPD). It is important to understand that I enjoyed my career. I enjoyed being a police officer and loved being a detective. Based on what I know today, if I could go back in time, I still would choose a career with the New York City Police Department. One of the first things to understand is that policing and being a police officer simply is a calling, it is "in" some of us. By "in," I mean, being a police officer is in our souls, is one of our dreams, and it is who we are. Most police officers are fulfilling their childhood dream.

This book will provide prospective law enforcement professionals the inside track on what to expect while working in law enforcement. The book will address questions about life in law enforcement and all it entails. However, this book will not cover such topics as police exams, the hiring process, specifics of academy training, racial issues, or the politics of the job. Instead, the book will go into detail about the money that can be made, the effects on family life, public sentiment, the camaraderie, the dangers and risks, and the way the "job" can change you as a person. There even is a chapter that provides reinforcement and reminders for anyone currently in a law enforcement career and advice for future law enforcement professionals. The chapter offers vital insight on tactics and getting through tough times.

Although my experiences derive from the NYPD, the topics and information presented here can be applied to other police departments and law enforcement agencies throughout the country. The term police officer and law enforcement professional are used repeatedly and interchangeably throughout the book. Both terms and the information presented here refer to all careers in law enforcement including police officer, detective, correction officer, special agent, or criminal justice counselor. This information can be used whether you are considering working in a small, medium-sized, or large agency. Many of the principles here also apply to local, state, and federal law enforcement agencies.

Law enforcement has similarities that stretch across the spectrum of the field. A police officer in a small town will confront many of the same personal and professional issues as does an officer in a huge metropolitan city. Issues here can even stretch across international lines. The only chapter that focuses heavily on the NYPD is Chapter one: Money, Retirement, and Benefits. To include all the different financial aspects of every police department and law enforcement agency in the United States would require ten books. However, the information therein should provide insight for law enforcement professionals in every department.

I was inspired to write this book because of the perceived mysteries and misconceptions associated with policing. Television and movies have presented a particular view of policing. It may be either positive or negative, but typically, it is an abbreviated version of just some of the issues that encompass the world of policing. As an Assistant Professor in Criminal Justice at John Jay College, I have the privilege of teaching and interacting with students who are intent on becoming some form of law enforcement officer. Through interaction with my students, I realize that the misconceptions are tremendous. I feel an obligation to present this inside look in attempts to educate and provide clarity.

Once these prospective officers and agents learn of my background in policing and my willingness to discuss my career in law enforcement, the series of questions begins and usually continues throughout the semester. This is a great privilege for me, as I feel it is my responsibility to answer questions and relate my experiences to the course curriculum. I begin every class with a question: "What do you guys want to talk about today?" This opens the floor to discussions of current events and life situations. I dedicate the first 10-15 minutes of every class to these open discussions, which usually range from politics to police shootings and protests, and everything else. The discussions can become so deep at times that I have to stop it because of time constraints. There are times that one topic or issue has been discussed in the first 10-15 minutes of each class for days and weeks. This is one of the benefits of being in a criminal justice class where the professor has law enforcement experience and is open to discussion.

My experience comes from 23 years in the NYPD, where I began in uniform, moved into plainclothes assignments, and then served in the Detective Bureau. My career with the NYPD was filled with thrilling and exhilarating moments in which I had the privilege of doing and being a part of amazing things - the type of things about which movies are made - but the best part, with which any police officer will agree, are the friends you make along the way. These friendships often become lifelong connections that never wither. The bonds that are forged are remarkable.

The attraction of policing is similar to an old United States Army commercial that used to play on television: "Be all you can be!" It certainly is true, the possibilities are endless. Every option is open in law enforcement. I had a student tell me that he wanted to join the NYPD because he hoped to be the Police Commissioner one day. The entire class laughed, but I told him that it is very possible that his dream will become a reality. It is strange and difficult to explain, the way so much is possible in policing, but it is. A police officer has the opportunity to work his way up through the ranks to become a Chief, a Detective, or anything in between. A police officer can work undercover on the streets, in the narcotics unit, the vice squad, or the gang unit, just to name a few. A person can even become an accountant, mortician, nurse, doctor, or lawyer during his/her law enforcement career. For the thrill-seekers, the options are open for the Emergency Service Unit (ESU) in NYPD, SWAT team in other states, Aviation, K-9, and Harbor. When I tell you that the sky is the limit, it is not a figure of speech. All you have to do is choose and then pursue your goal.

This book will highlight the various aspects of being in law enforcement. I would not call them good or bad issues, just issues and things you need to be aware of and expect. Law enforcement and policing can be difficult and challenging, and I think everyone knows and expects that. However, there are some things that you should clearly understand clearly before you choose this career. This book does not address political, racial or gender issues, or the inner workings of law enforcement agencies. It focuses instead on the personal issues

associated with being a law enforcement professional.

Chapter 1

Money, Retirement, & Benefits

Although I understand that many believe that there is no amount of money that will ever be enough for putting on a police uniform and risking their lives to protect others and uphold the law, there are those of us who feel it is a calling. Parents, family, and spouses of the men and women who choose this career often say they have difficulty understanding the choice their loved one has made. However, they often explain that it has been a lifelong dream, a calling they had to pursue, follow, and achieve. Many who choose this path

18

have it in their blood, in their psyche; it is who they are. Many would do it for no money if it weren't for life's financial obligations. Understanding the financial side of policing helps shed some light on some of the benefits associated with this challenging career choice.

Money is one of the misconceptions in policing, especially in larger cities like New York. This chapter of the book covers salaries and financial benefits specific to the NYPD, although I believe they may be similar in other large agencies and departments. As of this printing, the starting base salary for an NYPD officer is $42,500 after completing the 6-month academy and $45,674 a year, including top base pay, longevity and holiday pay, uniform allowance, and average night shift differential (NYPD Recruit.com, 2018). Yes, I agree, when you consider the risks and sacrifices associated with being a police officer, it is a low starting salary; however many young people today, even those with a college education, have a difficult time finding a first job with a starting salary of $45,674 when they graduate. However, do not be fooled by this salary. There are several very important factors to consider here, many that go beyond financial compensation, some that will be discussed in this book.

First and foremost, anyone entering the NYPD should be aware that, although the salary may start low, it increases into the six figures. The facts are as follows: the salary stated does not include overtime. Here is a look at how the extras can stack up for a slightly active new officer who does 10 hours per week overtime for 40 out of the 52 weeks per year:

Overtime (assuming 10hrs/wk @ 40 wks) =

$12,260

With the overtime added, a new officer can make approximately $55k-$60k during the first year. Even though not directly financial, becoming an NYPD officer includes unlimited sick leave with full pay, health insurance, including dental and vision (including options in which there is no cost to the member).

After 5 ½ years of service, an NYPD patrol officer is paid a base salary of $85,292 which translates into $91,998 with longevity and holiday pay, uniform allowance, and average night shift differential. This does not include overtime, which works out to:

Overtime (assuming 10 hours per week for 40 weeks) = $24,000 per year. This translates into a salary of approximately $116,000 for an officer with 5½ years on the job, in addition to the free medical, dental, and vision options, and unlimited paid sick leave. Another benefit that the NYPD provides its officers is a Neighborhood Policing salary enhancement which translates to an additional 2.25% of the base salary of officers who accept neighborhood policing assignments in the area in which they work.

The salary can increase rather quickly after officers reach top pay (5½ years). The salaries for patrol officers with over ten years on the job can be in the range of $130,000 to 150,000/year not to mention the differences that can occur within the various ranks. Do not fail to recognize that the rank and promotional opportunities within the policing profession provide extra incentives, financial rewards, and the opportunity for an increased retirement pension. When overtime, holiday pay, night differential, and longevity are added

to the base top salaries, the amounts are pretty attractive.

It also is important to understand that some Police

Departments other than the NYPD have additional

ranks.

Another very important aspect of a policing

career is the retirement benefits. NYPD officers of all

ranks earn a pension of half (50%) of their final year's or

the average of the final three year's salary, for the rest of

their lives. Although a portion of the police officers'

salaries (approximately 5%) is contributed to their

pension account, the city contributes the remaining

amount. The pension can translate into an astronomical

amount of money. Given that the average police officer

joins the police department before the age of 25

(Greenhut, 2014) and is therefore eligible for retirement

before age 50, and the average life expectancy of police officers is age 80 (Greenhut, 2014), that is over thirty years of pension payment. At a pension of $75,000 per year, calculated at 50% of a $150,000 final year salary, plus the $12,000 annual variable supplement, an average pension would be approximately $87,000 per year. Over 30 years, that equal $2.6 million in retirement income over an average lifetime. The police pension allows retired officers to have a lifetime income while staying home and relaxing, starting a second career, or opening a business. Because you have such an income, you can pursue whatever your heart desires, whatever you love to do, or you can explore interests you always wanted to. The possibilities are endless.

I feel I should provide an explanation of the variable supplement, as it was included in the pension calculations. The variable supplement is a $12,000 supplement that retired officers receive every December, before Christmas. According to a 2009 report by the State of New York Insurance Department, the variable supplement dates back to 1970 during Mayor Lindsay's administration, when the city borrowed money from the Police, Corrections, and Fire Department unions during a time of budget crisis when the city was near bankruptcy. The agreement indicated that the city would pay back the loan in the form of a variable supplement that started at $2,500 in 1988 and rose by $500 annually until it reached its maximum, $12,000 in 2007. This variable supplement is paid to every police officer hired after July 1, 1988, regardless of rank, who retires with 20 years of service and is paid for his or her lifetime. This is in addition to the regular pension; however, disability pensions are not eligible to receive the variable supplement. Further, under the Deferred Retirement Option Program (DROP), the annual variable supplement for police officers who remain employed with the NYPD beyond the twenty-year minimum will be banked for each year. Therefore, a police officer who retires after 25 years of service will have $60,000 banked, which he/she can choose to withdraw upon retirement or roll into one of the many other retirement options.

Continuing on the retirement income topic, there are several other retirement options. NYPD police officers can contribute to a New York City deferred compensation plan, a 401k plan, or an IRA account, and can make increased contributions to their pension accounts. In addition, the city contributes $522 per year (figures accurate as of 2013) into an annuity fund for every officer, to which they make no contributions. This annuity is invested over the twenty plus years and is available upon retirement or can be rolled into another retirement vehicle (NYC PBA Health & Welfare Benefits Bulletin, 2013).

Thus, as you can see, the financial benefits of being a police officer can be great. I personally know several police officers who have retired as millionaires, and this is not uncommon. However, the majority whom I've known personally, in various ranks, retire with retirement savings accounts in the vicinity of $350,000 to over $500,000. All of this retirement money is in addition to the lifetime pension that comes month after month, and the variable supplement, that comes year after year.

The income and retirement potential are just some of the benefits of becoming a NYPD police officer. There are many more benefits including options that provide assistance to veterans and military personnel, over 60 scholarships for continuing education for law enforcement officers (NYPD Scholarship Program, 2015), and programs for housing and homebuyers. I myself applied for, and was awarded a NYPD Educational Leave department scholarship that helped me earn my master's degree. The scholarship gave me nine paid days off per semester (18 days off to study per academic year) while attending school. The school at which I earned my master's degree had an NYPD Cohort program in which the graduate tuition was reduced by over 30% per credit, and the classes met once a week in the Police Academy. This is one example

28

of an NYPD scholarship, however there are many others, including financial and leave scholarships for undergraduate and graduate study and law school. This includes full scholarships and leaves of absence granted to attend programs out of state. Through my years of continuous interaction with the NYPD scholarship unit, I was asked repeatedly to inform my colleagues of the scholarship opportunities available because the majority of them go unused and cause some of the schools and organizations to threaten to redirect the funding to other areas. Therefore, if education is your goal, the NYPD is able to help.

There are also vacation time and time off benefits. NYPD police officers have the benefit of earning and accruing a considerable amount of time off per year. Recruits begin with ten vacation days per year.

That number increases through the completion of five years of service when vacation days increase to 27 days. That translates to over five weeks of vacation per year. In addition to vacation days, there are chart days. Chart days are an accumulation of time each police officer earns for working beyond the number of hours required per week. Police officers work different tours or charts. The chart could be a nine-hour tour, five days a week, a ten-hour tour, four days a week, or any other variation. Each chart has built-in chart days that accumulate and are returned to the member. Depending on the chart, it is not unusual for a police officer to have eight extra days off a year built into his/her chart in addition to the 27 vacation days earned.

Finally, there is accrued time earned through overtime. A police officer can be paid overtime in cash or time, which is earned at 1.5 times the hours worked. Overtime taken in time allows the police officer to use the accrued time for additional days off. For example, if an officer works 5 hours overtime, he/she has the option to take the overtime in cash or time. Regardless of the choice made, all overtime is earned at time and a half. Therefore, the five hours of overtime translate to seven and half hours in cash or time. As if this wasn't already a great option, a police officer has the option of splitting his/her overtime between cash and time. This means that the five hours overtime can be split into three hours cash and two hours time, all earned at time and a half. The time is banked and accrues as you continue to add more hours to the bank. This allows the police officer to take time off using vacation days, chart days, or time accrued.

It is clear that the financial benefits are significant, and when the time off is added, they're magnificent. Most people are not aware of all of these benefits. However, it wouldn't be fair if I painted only a pretty picture of all of this. There are some issues that must be included concerning vacation time and other time off.

The weeks you choose to take your vacation, are allotted by seniority. Therefore, a newer officer will have the opportunity to pick the weeks he wants for vacation last. This often means that the summer months and all the holiday weeks will be taken already by officers who have more seniority and had the opportunity to choose their vacation first. This will change as your time on the job increases, giving you better seniority. It's something to look forward to. I recall being last to pick vacation when I started, and then remember being first; it's a rite of passage.

The other issue that must be mentioned is that some working charts require that the member give back days. What this means is that because of the chart or hours you work, you owe working days back to the city. The 4X2 detective chart is one example. Although many detective units have moved away from using this chart; when used it meant that each detective would have to work two days per year without pay. It's not the best scenario, but the chart days often were completed at the shooting range, some other training session, or by surrendering two vacation days. It is one of those things that you have to learn to accept. However, in the overall scheme of things, I always saw it as a small price to pay, considering all the other great benefits there were.

Hopefully, the information above provides insight into the type of income that is possible in law enforcement. Detailed here is entry-level information; remember additional ranks and promotions can be earned in law enforcement, which will raise the benefits highlighted here.

Chapter 2

Respect and Envy

I want to start this chapter by saying that there are many people who love the police. I feel the need to make that statement because general public sentiment and the media would have you believe otherwise. Based on the protests throughout the country related to civil rights violations issues and the way media portrays and covers these protest, it may appear that the entire country hates the police. This is not the case. Most law-abiding citizens understand the need for an entity to uphold the laws created. Most understand that, without the police, there would be chaos, disorder, and pandemonium in the streets.

In addition to those who understand the need and purpose of the police, there are those who have family who are police officers. In fact, there are generations of police officers in some families. These families usually understand the life of a police officer well, the situations with which they cope, and what the work entails. These are the people who respect the police the most. When you mention the police, they often will begin to tell you about the past and current generations of family members who were, are, or are planning to become police officers. They are very proud of their family members and their family's heritage within the police department. They are quick to tell you about the ranks reached, the units they've been in, and the accomplishments their family members have achieved. They are very proud and are our greatest supporters.

However, even those who respect, understand the need for, and admire law enforcement, still do not understand what it is to *be* in law enforcement. They will never understand what you have seen or have experienced as an officer. They will not be able to understand the pain, the disappointment, and the hurt that sometimes are associated with being a police officer. I have spoken to many people who are amazed by the fact that I was an NYPD Homicide Detective. They are overwhelmed when they think of the things I have seen, the type of people I have dealt with, and that I was part of the biggest, largest, and finest police departments in the country. During these conversations, all I can think of saying is: You have no idea!

However, many people do not support or even appreciate the police because of their interactions with them. Most of the time, police interaction is related to a violation or a crime committed, being a victim, or some form of assistance. Thus, the majority of police contact is related to a negative or stressful situation. These contacts can leave the public with negative impressions about the police officer who stopped them, issued them a summons, or affected an arrest. When someone is being issued a summons or being arrested and they ask the officer if he/she could give them a break, and the officer is unable to oblige, the respondent is very likely to hold some form of animosity toward that officer. That feeling is magnified and multiplied when the person tells friends and family, as they all recall times when they were in similar situations and were not given a break. This resentment multiplies further when the police stop the respondent a second or third time. The feeling continues to grow when they see someone else pulled over on the side of the road by the police; it can be never-ending.

The types of persons who are usually envious of the police are those who had a desire to become police officers or law enforcement and for whatever reason could not. I first learned of and was warned about this type of person in the police academy, it was explained there are more people like this than most realize. Don't get me wrong; I am not saying that everyone that fits into this category feels this way. Many have gone on to excellent careers and lives; in fact, some look at not getting hired into law enforcement as a blessing for their particular lives.

However, this envious person is the guy or girl, who took the written exam and did not pass, passed the written exam and went through the hiring process and was disqualified, or because of their arrest history or other background issue knew they could not qualify. Not only is this person envious, but they can also have animosity towards the police. The animosity that exists is more significant amongst those who initiated the steps to join a department or agency and failed. In many instances their families, friends, and loved ones were aware when they were attempting to enter law enforcement; and they know they did not make it. This person's ego is tarnished; their resentment towards the police is stirred every time they come in contact with an officer. Once you are made aware that you are dealing with a person like this, be careful. They may not always want to see the best for you.

Then you have those who hate all police officers just because of what they stand for: justice; freedom; rules; restrictions, etc. Those who hate the police question the fact that any person should have the power to control or regulate the movement and freedoms of anyone else. Those who feel this way do not agree with the authority placed upon certain individuals just because they've passed a series of exams and test. It bothers them that a uniform, a badge, and a gun give a human being authority over another, especially the power to arrest and lock someone away from society. I have seen and dealt with these kinds of people on numerous occasions. They tend to look down on an officer of any rank and views them as a weak, cowardly person who could not survive in the world without the authority and power given by his/her position. There is no winning a verbal argument with this type of person. Your best course of action is to learn to ignore such people and just do your job.

In the academy, we were taught to never let anyone "Hook your Child!" This meant to never allow anyone to bring you down to the level where you act like a child. Maintain your adult and professional behavior in all situations. This brings to mind the photos of protestors yelling and screaming in a police officer's face while the officer stands tall at his/her post, unaffected externally by the protestor's abuse. Such officers refuse to allow the protestors to reduce them from a professional level down to that of a child who battles verbally or physically with such a person. Don't get me wrong; it is not an easy task to deal with an angry

protestor, and some of the words cut deep and hurt.

However, you must be prepared for this. As a law

enforcement professional in a city like New York City, a

tough city where the people are rough and hard on a

daily basis, you need to become accustomed to dealing

with and controlling your emotions from the outset.

Being a hot-head or having a low tolerance in these

situations could be detrimental to your health, wellbeing,

and to your career. Now if the tirade becomes physical;

if the protestor puts one hand on you, then all bets are

off! As a law enforcement professional, you have the

power and authority to stop the threat and make an arrest

when appropriate.

I use the phrase, "when appropriate" because

based on the situation and the violation or criminal act,

arrest may not be the order of the day. In New York City, and probably most cities, it is not always prudent to make an arrest for every breach of the law. It usually is the Sergeant, Lieutenant, Captain, or higher executive who will make the decision on the scene. In fact, in some situations, the decision is made in advance by police executives at the highest levels. Now, don't get me wrong; that doesn't mean that you will be instructed to take abuse or allow yourself to be assaulted - not at all. However, it could mean that you may be expected to use another course of action to avert the possibility that the situation will escalate to the point at which an arrest is required. In the case of a verbally aggressive protestor, what it could mean is that you may be instructed to restrain and then release the protestor or issue a summons, or the supervisor may rotate or shift officers to and from the front line to allow tempers to calm and patience to be restored. However, if anyone lays their hands on or spits on an officer, an arrest for assault on an officer is in order, bottom-line. There should be no exceptions in this situation.

Chapter 3

Camaraderie and Friendships

One of the best things about being in law enforcement is some of the people with whom you have the pleasure to work. I have met great people while working in the NYPD, from the custodial and clerical staff to police officers and detectives, and all the way up to chiefs. There is a camaraderie that exists among law enforcement professionals that extends far and wide. In addition to the usual commonalities that exist between persons who share the same childhood career dreams and goals, there is an extra bond that can exist between men and women who risks their lives together every day. If you add the fact that the shared risk is taken in the name of justice, law, and the common good, that bond is stronger than ever.

When officers are on the streets, working in some of the toughest areas and neighborhoods in the country, they know that if something goes awry, the only people they can rely on are other officers. When an officer puts out a call for help over the radio, only officers are responding, and they are coming full speed, no holds barred, to assist, fight for, help, and rescue their comrade. One of their brothers or sisters is in a life and death situation and needs help. Not only is this the position he/she is in because of the oath taken to protect, ninety percent of the time, officers initiate the contact and step up to an individual who committed some form of wrong. In a situation in which most people would turn

47

and run, officers puts their lives on the line, and risk not going home at the end of the night to their families, all to stop a wrong, to protect someone they don't know. For such men and women, we will risk our lives to get to them - to help.

I remember incidents from the beginning, after field-training, during my first days and weeks on the job, working with the NYC Transit Police, pre-merge. I was assigned to the Tactical Patrol Force, where the headquarters and roll calls were held in the 42nd Street/Times Square subway station. This was not an above-ground police station, but an underground police station, in the maze of subway stations and tunnels underground. The subway system under Times Square in Manhattan is another world. Millions of people pass through there every day, homeless people live there, and criminals and crime thrives.

While at roll call, there often would be "officer needs assistance" radio calls from officers in some part of the huge station. These bone-chilling calls, sometimes screams for help, would cause complete silence. Once the radio operator (central) determined the officer's location, the entire command would empty, and there would be 20-30 officers running full-speed through the Times Square station en-route to the officer in need. It was insane. Passengers traveling through the station would dive and maneuver to get out of our way. We gave it everything we had; nothing was going to stop us from getting to our brother or sister in need. We had no idea who the officer was and it did not matter; he or she was blue. That is all that mattered.

This is a bond that most cannot understand or imagine. Unless you can see yourself in that same position, unless you can see yourself as that officer risking everything to do right and having things go wrong. Unless you can see yourself in a near death situation, when the shit hits the fan, screaming or yelling for help over the radio, and praying that someone is coming… you will never truly understand. When that call comes over the radio, the voice of an officer in fear, it sends chills up your spine and gives you goose bumps all over.

When you've been on either side of that scenario several times, you learn very quickly who you have to rely. You learn very quickly that no matter what conflict, difficulty, or disagreement you may have had with a fellow officer, he/she still has your back, will still come running full speed or driving like a madman to help you, and you will do the same for him or her. That forges a unique level of camaraderie. This camaraderie last forever; it forges a bond that can be as strong as or stronger than family bonds because it involves life and death.

This is the part of police work that often mimics what we see on television and in the movies. Police officers, especially partners, often are in a position in which their lives depend upon each other. In everyday situations, officers have each other's backs. They make plans to carry out assignments, set up signals to alert each other when there is trouble, and protect each other in any way necessary.

The camaraderie described here goes far beyond physical safety and protection. The camaraderie often extends beyond race, religion, and background. There are many officers who become God-parents to their partner's child, best man, maid-of-honor, organ donor, etc. Police officers, especially those who work together, have a responsibility to assure the wellbeing of their fellow brothers and sisters in blue. Well-being includes mental health, alcohol and substance abuse, as well as family and relationship issues. Because of the stress and complexities associated with being a police officer of any designation or rank, external issues and temptations can be detrimental. It is important that police officers do their best to keep a clear mind, body, and spirit. Doing their best includes taking care of themselves and watching for signs that another officer is dealing with stress or issues that could affect his/her performance, mental outlook, or wellbeing.

Added to that camaraderie are the fun times that are created. The times when silly things are done, like turning an officer's locker upside down in the locker room, putting it in the parking lot or the subway platform, putting things in an officer's desk drawer, or simply the funny things that occur on the street. An incident comes to mind where I was driving a police car. Let me start by saying that I am and have always been an excellent driver. However, driving a police car, with lights and sirens on, dodging traffic and pedestrians in an emergency, is a very different thing.

So, it was a few years after the merger of the NYPD with the Transit and Housing Police Departments. I was new in the Manhattan Robbery Squad's - Transit Robbery Squad, a detective unit that investigated subway crimes. I had just come from

Transit Anti-Crime and spending my whole early career in the Transit Police Department. This pretty much meant that I spent most of my career, up until this point, underground policing the subways. The first and last time I drove a police car under emergency situations was in the police academy. An early call came in from patrol notifying the office that there were multiple people stabbed at a subway station across town and street cops were holding the train and all witness at the scene. This was big, not only because there were multiple people stabbed, but because the police on the scene were making the NYC Metropolitan Transit Authority hold the train, during rush-hour; an event that could cause major train delays system-wide.

Because it was early, I was the only one in the office other than the Sergeant and the Lieutenant. We knew what we had to do. The Sergeant tossed me the keys, we ran upstairs, and jumped into one of the unmarked police cars that were assigned to our office. It was the height of the morning rush hour in Manhattan and I was driving. Remember, at this point, I had never driven a police car on public streets, marked or unmarked; let alone in Manhattan during rush-hour. Even with the vehicle's lights and sirens on, we had delays at the traffic lights and intersections and would become stuck in traffic. So I thought, hey we're the police! I'll go around all of this! I realized that there were no vehicles parked along the curb of the street and I turned the vehicle towards the curb and began to drive to the right of all the vehicles stuck in the rush-hour traffic. Now mind you, I'm driving on the street, not the sidewalk. What I did not realize is that I was supposed to go to the left, cross the double yellow line, and cautiously proceed towards on-coming traffic that would see me and move out of my way.

Well, I didn't. There were pedestrians stepping off the sidewalk who were alarmed and startled when they realized a speeding unmarked police car with lights and sirens was hastily approaching them. Some pedestrians jumped back, some fell back, and many were screaming. My bosses, who were both NYPD street cops who had become supervisors, were in the car with me yelling, covering their faces, bracing themselves, and I think I even saw feet on the dashboard! I learned how to drive a police car during an emergency response in a busy city that day. Thankfully, no one was hurt or injured. However, I received months of embarrassing ridicule from everyone as the story was repeated at every opportunity. My supervisors laughed at me, the situation we were in, and the fact that they had no idea I had never driven a police vehicle in an emergency. I laughed at myself as I tried to explain.

After that incident, in future emergency responses throughout my career, every time I had to cross the double yellow line and proceed towards on-coming traffic, I would chuckle. In fact, to this day those same supervisors, whom I still maintain a friendship with, bring it up and we all laugh. Fortunately for me, and to show that many situations have a good and bad side; it was the way I handled this particular case and the writing in my paperwork that first gained the attention of the Manhattan South Homicide Squad, where eventually became a member. Every officer has stories that have created laughter and great memories.

Along with the camaraderie among the great men and women you work with, you will make bonds with other great people who you'll meet as a result of a variety of circumstances. There will be victims and their families, perpetrators and their families, and regular citizens that will make a connection with you that will change your life and theirs, and that will last a lifetime.

One particular case comes to mind which shows the incredible bonds and friendships that can be established as a result of a tragedy. To respect the privacy of the family, I will not get into the details or the facts surrounding the tragedy and the events that followed. It started in 2011, when a passenger helicopter and its four passengers crashed into the East River at the 34th Street heliport in New York City, shortly after take-off. Ultimately, the pilot and one passenger survived the crash. My office and I got involved due to a variety of reasons: 1) technically, it would have to be investigated as a homicide until details and facts determine otherwise, 2) there are survivors who must be interviewed and both investigative and hostage negotiation skills could be beneficial, and 3) the proximity of the crash to the homicide office made us the obvious senior investigative unit for response. So my office responds, some to the scene and some to the hospital. The case is mine, so I respond to the hospital with my supervisor. The mindset here is: male and female investigators, both HNT certified; together they can handle any variation of things that come their way. As the facts begin to come in from the scene and the hospital, and the status of the passengers are obtained, it becomes my responsibility to begin an initial light interview with the survivors, where possible, and the notification of death, if and when appropriate. It is here that an incredible, life-long bond was made.

Once my supervisor and I arrived at New York University (NYU) hospital, the hospital staff informed us that one passenger had died, two were in critical condition, and one survived and was conscious, along with the pilot. We did not want to speak with the pilot at this point and focused on the conscious survivor. The hospital staff informed us that the conscious passenger was a male tourist from Portugal, the husband, and father of the family and that the helicopter ride was to be a sightseeing excursion to see the statue of liberty and the NYC skyline from above. They explained that he was still shaken and was sitting in the Emergency Unit's family waiting area, conferring with the hospital's social workers. This initially shocked us; shouldn't he at least be in a hospital bed? This man was just pulled from the East River after a helicopter crash; the fact that he was not sedated, medicated, or in a hospital bed told us a lot about him from the start. I entered the doorway of the small waiting area and observed the scene for a moment. He was an upper-middle-aged man, wearing hospital clothing because his were wet and removed by hospital personnel. He was sitting alone, with tears in his eyes, and obviously shaken. There were three hospital social workers standing around him repeatedly asking him questions about what happened and how he felt. We decided to walk in, and I sat next to him. I held his hand with both of mine, and he looked at me. We locked eyes for a moment, at which time I asked the social worker staff to leave the room. They stopped their inquiry and looked at me like I was crazy. I explained that they are welcomed to wait outside the room and return once we are done. Surprisingly they did not put up a fight. I believe that when I walked in, sat next to him, and held his hand, the message was clear.

Once they left the room, I reached over and hugged him. The embrace from him was strong and lasting; I felt his pain. The details of this tragedy reminded me of the many vacations I've taken with my family where we go on tourist excursions to sightsee or experience the culture and customs of the area. The glass bottom boat, jet-skis, parasailing, snorkeling, zip-lining, ATV tours, bus tours, horseback riding, and many others. It was easy to place myself in this gentleman's shoes; it could have easily have been me. I sat there with my supervisor, providing comfort to the gentleman, and the only thing he wants to know is why he is sitting here alone and where is his family. After repeatedly attempting to divert his line of questioning to the detail and fact-finding questions I was supposed to lead into, I realized I could not avert the obvious task in front of me any longer. I held both of his hands now, as tight as I could, looked into his already tear-filled eyes and told him that of his family, he was the only one who was not hurt. I told him that his daughter did not make it and that his wife and the other passenger were in critical condition. It was an enormous, heartfelt task, which had all of us in tears. Even if the situation he found himself in, sitting there alone, created the possibility of hope in his mind, there was none now. I had taken that away.

I had done many notifications over throughout my career, but this was a tough one. The emotion and connection that I shared with this gentleman, who was now alone in this country, made us close. I did not want to leave this man's side. I was him; he was me. It was incredible, the city and the mayor's office got involved and allowed us to be assigned to him and his family as they arrived. A businessman donated a furnished luxury apartment in Manhattan for use by the family while they spent time in the United States and traveled to and from the hospital for over a month. My supervisor and I became extremely close to him and the entire family.

It was later learned that the other passenger was a close friend of the family. Through several miracles that occurred, the hospital was able to maintain life support of his wife and the close family friend. Although they were not conscious, it allowed the gentleman the opportunity to see them. Unfortunately, the family friend died shortly after, as the result of her injuries. In a miracle, as I have never experienced, after several weeks, while his wife remained unconscious, with family and friends arriving from across the seas, and the incredible public outpour of affection, she awakens! The hospital could not even explain it. She woke and was able to talk, smile, and communicate. The husband was ecstatic as would be expected. We would visit, and he'd smile for the first time since we met him. My supervisor and I, as well as other detectives who became involved in the case, were introduced and had conversations with his wife. Unfortunately, one night while sleeping in the hospital, she passed away. It was a difficult miracle, but it allowed the gentleman the opportunity to spend time with his wife, one last time. How amazing is that? Although it is an obvious tragedy that she was lost, imagine the opportunity to get someone back, even for a day or two. The things you would say to them! The things you would show them!

The friendship and bond that was created between us, the gentlemen and his family have been tremendous. They have visited the United States several times where we've spent time together, we've communicated via telephone and social media regularly, we send birthday and holiday greetings, and we have congratulated each other on our endeavors and successes throughout the years. We honestly see ourselves as a family. We became so close during the month or so that they were here. This lifetime closeness was built through a connection that occurred as a result of a career in the NYPD.

Chapter 4

Satisfaction

Becoming a police officer in New York City comes with many benefits and exciting times. There also is a certain satisfaction in knowing that you actually are making a difference in the world, a difference in society, a difference in someone's life. Although I can't speak for all police officers, I can say that most of the officers I've spoken to, worked with, or known over the years have indicated either verbally or through their actions that they entered law enforcement to help people. Some are more passionate than are others, and some are committed openly, while others mask their true feelings and passions.

Regardless of the level of enthusiasm the officer exhibits, the satisfaction that occurs when an officer or detective saves a life, arrests an individual who is accused of committing a heinous crime, or locates a missing child or person is greater than most can understand. The satisfaction from being responsible solely or as part of the team for removing a criminal from the streets, putting the handcuffs on the suspect, participating in a trial in which the suspect was found guilty, obtaining justice for the victim, and saving the world from being future victims, is unmatched and makes it all worthwhile.

I recall a case in which I participated while working in the Manhattan South Homicide Squad. It was an emotional case for all involved. The family was distraught, the public was terrified, the media were all over it, and the detectives investigating the case were submerged deeply in this horrific crime. During the investigation, there were many meetings during which the different units and detectives involved in the case would come together to discuss the developments and strategize plans to identify and locate the perpetrator. At every meeting, you could see the seriousness in everyone's face and demeanor; no one was taking this case lightly. One of my partners from my office stated, "I hope I'm the one who gets to put the cuffs on the perp." It was clear that everyone agreed and felt the same way, but they asked why anyway. My partner replied, "You'll see." When the day came that the perpetrator was identified and located, my partner was lucky enough to be the one who was responsible for handcuffing the perpetrator. As he cuffed him he stated," _____ _____, you are under arrest for the homicide of _____ _____." Just like in the movies, everyone involved in the case felt the incredible satisfaction, and my partner's satisfaction was unparalleled.

Most people see the news reports of a crime or read the story in the newspaper. They say to themselves, their families, or friends: "I hope *they* get that bastard" while thinking at the same time that they hope the perpetrator doesn't come to the area where they live or get one of their family members. The *they* to whom they are referencing is us: the police. Most will not do what we do; most do not even want to do what we do; however, we do it every day.

Another incident that comes to mind is an HNT job in which I was the lead. The job involved a young male, 25- 35 years old, who was standing on the outside of one of the bridges between the boroughs of Brooklyn and Manhattan in New York City threatening to jump. The request for my response came via telephone to my office at the Manhattan South Homicide Squad informing me of the details and that ESU was already on the scene. I put on my HNT jacket, ran out to the unmarked police vehicle, hit the lights and siren, and sped towards the scene. The first problem became apparent as soon as I got about 300 feet onto the bridge. Traffic came to a complete standstill. ESU had closed the bridge to vehicular and pedestrian traffic on the Manhattan side, which is protocol. In Manhattan, in many instances, when the streets are closed, there is nowhere to go, you simply sit and wait. Therefore, the lights and sirens were doing me no good; I wasn't going anywhere. I immediately pulled the vehicle over, got out, and began walking up the bridge, and because I was on the vehicular roadway, I had to climb maintenance ladders and use access walkways to get to the pedestrian walkway where this HNT job was.

As I got closer, I could see the police patrol and ESU personnel on the bridge's pedestrian walkway. Once I arrived, a chief and several supervisors approached me to bring me up to speed on the incident. I was informed that the individual on the outside of the bridge entered from the Brooklyn side, climbed over the retaining bars and gates, and is standing on a very narrow ledge, holding on with his two hands. The male is threatening to jump because the relationship with his girlfriend has ended, she hates him, and he doesn't want to live anymore. The bosses informed me that ESU has been talking to the male for about 30 minutes and are not making headway. At this point, they were not aware of his name or any of the specifics related to the male in distress.

I informed the bosses that I would attempt to establish a rapport with the individual and get him to come off the ledge and back over to the pedestrian walkway. The ESU boss then came over with very explicit instructions for me. He first made it clear that where the male had moved to and is currently standing is not visible from the pedestrian walkway. He explained that for me to be able to talk with the male, I'd have to be tied and anchored down by the ESU team, in case the male grabs for me as he jumps off the bridge, I won't go with him. The ESU boss asked whether I was alright with that requirement. I paused for short moment to make sense of what I was just told and said, "I'm good."

His second instruction began with him telling me that there are two ESU members hanging by ropes off the side of the bridge about 10-20 feet on both sides of the male. The instruction was that I was to make no mention of them while talking to the male. He explained that the male is agitated by the two ESU men and it has caused him to move from the accessible area he was originally standing into the inaccessible area where he is standing now. The ESU boss further explained that the goal is to shift the male's thoughts and attention away from the two ESU men and onto me. I gestured that I understood.

The final instruction from the ESU boss was that although the male had climbed onto the ledge on his own, there was no way that they could let him climb back over to the pedestrian walkway on his own. He made it clear that this meant that the two ESU guys would have to make contact with him and assist or carry him back over to the pedestrian walkway and safety. He explained that it would be a disaster if you get him to come back in and he falls to his death while climbing the gates to get back to the pedestrian walkway. I agreed. The ESU boss added that it could either be a rescue or an assist and that will be determined by progress and opportunity.

So, I got harnessed in and tied around my waist and then approached the edge of the bridge. I partially climbed over the first barrier, and I hear a voice say

"Stop!" It was the ESU boss advising me to move slowly. I proceed slowly and tug on the rope which is anchoring me; this is to signal the ESU member holding it that this is the point where I stop, and where tension should be maintained. I begin a dialogue with the male who is extremely upset and agitated about the police presence. It actually takes some time to get him back to the issue that has us all assembled here. However, in time his attention is all mines. I dig at first to make sure I understand his issues, I then relate, and discuss similar situations from my life with the specific solutions that were successful. As the male began to become more engaged in our conversation, I could see the two ESU men signaling each other and moving in. I cautiously and secretively signaled them to stop. I was making great headway; I knew I had him. However, I remembered the instructions from the ESU boss;

regardless of how this ends, he cannot climb back over

on his own. I refocused on the conversation and let the

ESU guys do their thing.

After about 30 minutes of deep conversation with

my new friend, he agreed to come back over to the

pedestrian walkway where we could maybe get a beer

and talk about our lives like gentlemen. I could see the

tremendous difference in his facial expressions and the

reduced tension in his body. It was like a weight lifted

off his shoulders. He was smiling, and I was smiling.

Then I remembered that I had to let him know that the

ESU guys would be helping him back up and over the

gates. I was so entrenched in the conversation that I

forgot they were there too. I knew this could destroy the

relationship I just built, could take the entire job back to

77

square one, or worse cause him to see me as a deceitful liar, just like all the rest, and jump to his death.

Just as I began to shift gears back to law enforcement mode to let him know about the ESU guys helping him back over; they swooped in and grabbed him. It was crazy; the way they swooped in it was like they flew from the sky directly into the bridge and just grabbed him. All of a sudden the slack in all of the ropes became tight, and I, my new friend, and the two ESU guys were hoisted back onto the bridge's walkway. It was like an amusement park ride, only real.

Patrol officers ran in and tackled the male. They secured him and transported him to the hospital for psychological evaluation. My job was done, except for the paperwork. We all shook hands, had a short debriefing on the bridge, re-opened vehicular and pedestrian traffic, and went on our separate ways. I visited my new friend in the hospital a few days later, and we talked for 30 minutes. He was happy and extremely thankful. I was also; things could have gone many different ways out there. I was happy and felt an enormous level of satisfaction to have the privilege of being involved at this level. It's indescribable.

Another day in New York City, another day in the life of the NYPD. I was proud, others were proud, it was good. This is what we do as police officers and law enforcement, the ESU guys do this level of rescue and saving lives every day. It has to be a calling; not everyone could do this.

Law enforcement professionals run to danger and violence while others run away. We stand and fight while others hide. I often think of a gun fight. When people hear gunshots, they duck and run, while the police charge towards the gunfire and fire back. Yes, we have guns and bulletproof vests, but those vests we wear don't cover our whole bodies; they don't cover our faces, our heads. Police take cover behind objects when cover is available and when there is none, we still respond. As a police officer, you will be saving lives and providing closure to victim's families and loved ones. With the exception of doctors and firemen, there are few people in this world who can say the same. You also will be one of the few people who openly risks your life to protect and save that of someone else. You will risk your life for someone who you do not know, someone who may not like you and what you stand for, a total stranger.

Another area in which satisfaction plays a role is the realization that police and law enforcement are living the life about which books, television programs, and movies are made. Regardless of where you work in law enforcement, you are accomplishing and reaching your goals. I recall driving into Manhattan on several occasions throughout my career. At a certain point in my commute, coming across the bridge or approaching the tunnel, I could see the New York City skyline ahead of me. I could see the skyscrapers, the World Trade Center, the Empire State building, the vehicles traveling along the Franklin D. Roosevelt (FDR) Drive, and the Harlem River Drive. When I reached the city, I'd see the hustle and bustle of the pedestrians, the yellow taxis, and the emergency personnel and vehicles with lights and sirens blaring, everywhere. A sudden feeling of accomplishment often came over me in these moments.

I'd often think, Wow, I'm a Homicide Detective

in New York City, Manhattan, in the greatest police department in the world. It started as a dream when I was a child, watching television programs and movies like *Shaft, Starsky & Hutch, Berretta, Magnum PI, CHiPs, Police Story, Adam-12, The Streets of San Francisco, The Rookies, S.W.A.T., Hawaii Five-O,* and *The Mod Squad.* It developed into a passion I had to pursue. It developed into a reality and a dream come true.

This is and can be true for you as well. The risks can be high, the sacrifices great, but the satisfaction cannot be described.

Chapter 5

New Awareness

One of the most interesting changes that will occur in you when you become a police officer is a new awareness that you will develop. This new awareness or vision is a heightened sense of perception, the ability to see things that others don't, to hear keywords in the conversations of those around you even when you don't realize you're listening, to notice the unusual in everyday occurrences, and to react quickly when danger is afoot. This new enhanced perceptual ability will keep you, your family, your friends, and those around you safe from danger and wrong doing. This heightened awareness will allow you to prepare and react in advance to maintain your safety in any situation.

The new awareness that you will gain as a police officer or law enforcement agent comes from the training at the academy, the lessons learned on the streets, and the countless victims who have or are experiencing the dangers of life. This will be a trait that you will never be able to unlearn, and will possess for the rest of your life. It will put you on edge, but in a good way. Your heightened vision will guide most of your movements both on duty and off duty. You, your friends, and your family will become used to your hyper-vigilance and expect it.

In the academy, you will learn the way criminals think, how to defend yourself in physical altercations, and most importantly how to see and hear danger before it becomes evident to most. You will master these lessons because they will save your life, allow you to avoid being caught off-guard in a bad situation, and allow you to run worst-case scenarios in your head to prepare for possible encounters. Your life will never be the same.

The change associated with this hyper-awareness goes far beyond the common practice of sitting facing the door in a restaurant or noting where the exits and windows are located wherever you go. Wherever you are you will notice when individuals exhibit unusual behavior. You will notice vehicles that do not belong in a particular setting for whatever reason. You will make a mental or written note of a suspicious person's description and the vehicle's color, make, model, and full or partial license plate numbers. You will notice the person or the vehicle that passes or circles around more than once, is hiding in the cut, or is sitting suspiciously in a car on your street.

You will be in a crowd at a party, a concert, or a sporting event and you will hear things. You will hear a portion of the details of an argument or a disagreement, which will cause you to remain alert and monitor the situation from afar. You will look for signs of increased intensity, persons leaving and returning from the location, and of course weapons. You will begin to identify who is together, on which side all the players are, and possibly which are the aggressors and leaders in the group.

You always will be in alert mode. Whether with family, friends, other cops, or loved ones, you always will be "on." You will be aware of your surroundings even when you take out the garbage, looking around constantly and absorbing everything in your surroundings. It may sound like a hassle or an unwanted obligation, but trust me, it's not. There is no thought involved. It is not a task or a job - it is a trait that will come naturally. It is who you will become subconsciously and you will appreciate it.

Your new awareness can be viewed as a blessing and a curse. If not handled correctly, it can ruin your ability to have a good time when out with family, friends, and loved ones, because it will have you always looking for trouble. Hopefully, it will cause you to decide to avoid situations or places potentially prone to crime, or associate with people who could be dangerous.

When there is any doubt that something untoward might

happen or that people with unclear motives are present,

it is best not to be there at all. Many have failed to learn

this lesson and have suffered the consequences by losing

their jobs and even ending up in jail.

One of the restrictions associated with being a

police officer is not to associate with known criminals or

persons known to participate in illegal activities.

Another restriction is being in locations where there are

known criminals or where illegal activities take place. If

these restrictions are followed, you more than likely will

be avoiding trouble. Remember, as a police officer and

law enforcement professional, associating with people or

places that are involved in criminal activities may be

against your agency's or department's internal policies regarding fraternization.

You do have to be careful about one aspect of the new perception you will gain, and I have seen it happen. It can cause you to be an angry and bitter person because you often observe and deal with bad people in bad situations, sometimes every day. It is easy for you as a police officer or law enforcement professional to begin to lose faith in society, to fail to be able to see the good in people, or the fact that good people exist. Your new awareness can develop into a restricted and stereotypical way with which you view the world. This blurred vision can affect the way you talk to and interact with the people you deal with every day and can make you a law enforcement professional who is so jaded that you cannot function in public.

Most departments and agencies offer sensitivity training to address this type of issue. The training can go by many different names and include a wide variety of other topics. It usually is mandatory training that is given periodically to meet the needs of the particular department and its members. The training is also available on a needs basis. In fact, this is one of the things that your supervisors should recognize through daily interactions or increased complaints. Your brothers and sisters in blue will also recognize if this change in you is too obscure. It is your partner's responsibility to speak with you, assess the situation, and help in any way they feel appropriate. However, if you feel yourself becoming this way, having these feelings, or if someone mentions it to you, inquire about the training as early as possible. I believe that being in this mental state for too long is problematic in many ways and can make it difficult for the officer to be retrained.

You do not want to be the officer who goes into every situation with preconceived notions; the officer who uses disrespectful and vulgar language on the streets when dealing with the public, in people's homes, in the courtroom, and in your own home in front of your family and loved ones. You do not want to be the officer who escalates every situation as soon as you arrive on the scene because your respect for humanity has been altered. You do not want to be the officer who no one can talk to.

Chapter 6
Family, Private Life & Public Sentiment

F amily should be considered in any discussion of a law enforcement career. This pertains not only to the safety issues, which will be discussed later, but I'd like to discuss here the strains involved with having, maintaining, and flourishing as a family unit while being a police officer.

In case you were unaware, being a police officer, especially in busy areas of the country like New York City, can impose a strain on family life. In fact, there are so many issues associated with police work and family life that clash, that when you enter the police academy, there are lessons for the officer and orientations for the families to help both parties acclimate better to the new lifestyle and allow them to recognize issues that are common in this career. This was very surprising to me when I first entered the police academy because I simply wanted to be a police officer. I never thought about all the other details and sacrifices that could be associated with my desire.

The information the academy provides is not a warning or a scare tactic in any way. It is designed to ensure that you and your family members are aware of the sacrifices that lie ahead for both parties and to inform both of the issues and problems that others have faced and coped with in this career. The hope is that the officers and their families can help each other through the process. The issues can be many, but when handled correctly, they can be addressed successfully. Again, we're not talking yet about the obvious dangers associated with being a police officer.

The first thing that you and your family should be prepared for is absence. Being a police officer is a 24-hour-a-day career. It's not like working in corporate America or being a school teacher, where you work 9 to 5, with weekends and holidays off. You cannot be sure you'll be home for dinner most evenings, and you probably won't be able to be your son's baseball or basketball team's coach. In fact, you will miss a lot of your children's and family's games, recitals, and birthdays, including your own. This is even more common during your first few years on the job when your seniority is low, and you're still considered a rookie who has to pay your dues. Paying dues in an around the clock police department means that someone has to work nights, holidays, and weekends. Guess who? This same mentality also applies to vacation picks – all of which are made based on seniority.

This way of doing things requires officers to accept the way things are, however, it is equally important that their families accept and understand the way things are also. It is difficult enough for officers to miss cherished family events, but the situation can be devastating when they have a spouse or family member who does not or refuses to understand. There has to be an understanding discussed from the beginning. The situation is problematic in itself, and it can become overwhelming without support. Police officers' spouses cannot be hounding them about when they're coming home, why they never come to their children's game, or are never available for their anniversaries or birthdays. These early issues simply cannot come between officers and their families. There must be an understanding of what a police officer has to do to achieve his/her goals and dreams.

Without the necessary understanding between all parties, the possibility of drinking, violence, or divorce exists. These are the dangers that accompany the stresses of the job. These stresses can destroy officers, make them slow to react, and take them off their game. This cannot happen! It creates a dangerous situation, not only for the officer but the public. If you have troubles on your mind while working and carrying a gun, it could lead to trouble. As a police officer, you have to be sharp and always ready to react to anything. I recall going to work on several occasions after dealing with a situation at home with family or in a relationship and being disconnected from work. It made for a tough day in which it was difficult to focus.

Privacy is critical when you become a police officer, regardless of where you work or live, and particularly if you work or live in one of the hot spots in the country where policing is under a magnifying glass. I'm referring to places like New York City, Los Angeles, Chicago, Baltimore, etc., cities where there are protests, high crime, and repeated conflict between the police and the communities they serve. It is especially difficult to be a police officer in these and others cities that experience similar climates.

The difficulty comes from the fact that a good number of the residents in areas with these issues do not like the police or feel that their methods are abusive, biased, and excessive. That argument will not be examined here, because this book is not written to explore the rights and wrongs in policing. I accept the fact that there are controversial issues between the police and the community, based on my experiences in New York City. It is issues like this that make it more important to conceal the fact that you are a police officer. When people find out that you are in law enforcement, you wait to see what their response will be before you proceed, as you never know what to expect.

When your law enforcement occupation is exposed, there are those who will thank you. Some will feel you are brave and will admire your desire to help others. Some will relate to you being in law enforcement because of family or friends they know in law enforcement or even their own desire to join the force and be a police officer at one point in their lives. There are those who will feel safer in your presence and will admire you for being able to protect your family and others. However, not everyone will feel that way.

You will encounter people who learn that you are in law enforcement and will want nothing to do with you. They will hate you immediately. There will be times when you will be talking to people, and the question of occupation comes up. You actually will see the expression on their faces change when you tell them what you do. I have run into friends from my youth whom I haven't seen in many years, guys whom I used to be pretty close to in our youth, tell me, "I heard you are 5-0 now! I can't mess with you no more!" and walk or drive away. I assumed they either were involved in something illegal or hate cops because of past

97

experiences. Either way, it wasn't a problem for me; I was content with my decision.

The privacy issue arises when you have to conceal consciously the fact that you are in law enforcement. One way, in particular, is related to social media, where it is best to post only a non-identifiable profile picture, limit your photos, or take extra care in accepting friend requests and allowing access to your page. All this is necessary to keep people out of your business and prevent them from knowing the details of your life and family. You will want to limit your exposure to the general public when it comes to who you are and what you do.

An example of what can occur is the numerous stories about employees who refuse to serve uniformed officers in businesses, or in which restaurant workers spit in, or poison, the food being made for or served to police. We hear these stories all the time. In fact, there are restaurants, fast food establishments, and delicatessens that police officers avoid.

Another privacy or safety issue involves your private vehicle. Some officers have had their cars spat on, scratched purposely, their tires flattened, and even obscenities spray painted across the hood, windshield, and doors. In fact, while I was still working, we were warned about people loosening the lug nuts on police cars and officer's private vehicles so that the vehicle's wheels came off while it was moving. This led to cameras being placed outside the precinct to monitor the vehicles. When I worked in Manhattan, there was a woman who lived on the same block as the precinct who hated cops. She rode around the city on an old bicycle. She hated the cops so much that she took the rubber grips off the handlebars to expose the metal ends. She would then squeeze herself and the bicycle between the parked police cars and private vehicles belonging to police officers and scratch them purposely. She got me twice. It was hard to detect when she was doing it, but the surveillance cameras installed on the block caught her finally, and she was arrested.

One safeguard I practice is to keep my private vehicle registered to a Post Office box. In this way, if someone sees my vehicle on the precinct block or sees me getting into or out of it while I'm off duty, and they take down my plate number to run it through DMV, they will not be able to determine where I live.

Chapter 7

The Dangers and Risks

Everyone knows policing is dangerous and there are many risks involved with the job. Well, let's talk about that. Many police officers go through their entire careers without ever having to use their weapon in the line of duty. However, most do have to remove their weapon from their holster several times during their careers. Doing so means that they either are in a situation in which they may have to shoot someone, or are in a situation where an armed individual may try to hurt them. The frequency with which you have to remove your weapon from its holster and use it depends on several factors.

The first factor, of course, is the location of your assignment. If you work in a tough part of town or the city, it is more likely that you will have to draw your weapon. The likelihood of approaching an armed robber, burglar, or being in an actual shootout are higher in certain areas. In New York City, there are areas where crime is higher and are more prone to violence than are others. These types of areas exist in almost every city in the United States.

You will know when you are working in one of these areas. The officers usually carry more than one gun, gun and drug arrests are high and occur daily, and the officers who work there gain a certain extra hardness and street savvy. If you work in one of these tough areas, you will learn to know the players, the hot spots, and the dangerous locales.

The second factor that will determine whether you will have to draw your gun or even use it is your assignment. If you're in certain units, you will have to remove your weapon from its holster, no question about it. If you are assigned to one of the high activity, specialized task forces within your police department, the likelihood will be high. By specialized I am referring to Anti-Crime units, Narcotics, Vice, and any other Task

Force in which the responsibility or objective is to address certain crimes as they occur.

Policing can be broken down into several different crime-fighting units, departments, areas, or bureaus, depending on the law enforcement agency. For the sake of simplicity, I will use the term sectors in this book. There are sectors that prevent crime, those that stop crimes and make arrests, sectors that investigate crimes after they occur, and those that support the other units. Most of these sectors can accomplish the goals of another when needed. Let me explain this a little more and how it relates to the dangers of the job.

Uniformed police patrols have an enforcement, response, and prevention role. This means that one of their objectives is to enforce the laws by issuing tickets and making arrests. They also are charged to respond to emergency calls and correct the situation once they arrive on the scene. That correction includes a multitude of different options and can range from providing first aid, quelling domestic violence, removing a disorderly patron, directing traffic at a broken traffic light, or stopping an armed robbery in progress. The uniformed patrol also includes a prevention objective. The police cars and the men and women in uniform provide omnipresence. Omnipresence allows the public to see the police and know that their safeguards are in place. Omnipresence also instills the fact that the police are there and watching, which prevents breaking the law, from committing minor violations like running red lights to more serious crimes.

As you can see, the uniformed patrol sector has broad objectives and responsibilities, and I've identified just some of them. This is why it is always the largest part of any police department. Most state and federal agencies do not share these objectives and responsibilities, as their functions are usually more specialized. Therefore, they do not have a large uniformed presence. Also apparent is how versatile the uniformed patrol sector of any police department must be. Officers must be able to shift from saving a life to taking a life at a second's notice.

The next sector that focuses on stopping crime and making arrests are the plainclothes and specialized units. The plainclothes units will work undercover in regular street clothing to address specific crimes. A unit like the narcotics unit will identify drug operations and then send in undercover officers to make buys or infiltrate the operations while collecting evidence and building a case. Such work ultimately will lead to making arrests. An anti-crime unit undertakes similar tasks. Anti-crime officers often blend in at public locations where specific crimes have been occurring. For example, a plainclothes anti-crime officer may ride the trains to look for pick-pockets and peruse drug stores and other retail locations to observe and apprehend shoplifters and thieves.

These units do not wear uniforms or write tickets. In such units, you are dealing with a different element of society all the time. That is the focus of your job. It is likely in a unit like one of these that you will have to remove your weapon from its holster often and perhaps even use it. There also is a greater likelihood that a suspect will flee or pull out a weapon to prevent being apprehended.

Another crime-fighting sector in most police departments is the detective bureau or unit. In the detective bureau, most crimes are investigated after the fact. This unit includes detectives who investigate larcenies, robberies, burglaries, sexual assaults, homicides, financial crimes, etc. Most cases in these units are initiated by patrol or reports of a crime that has occurred already. Detectives then take a case and begin an investigation to ascertain the perpetrator's identity and location.

In these types of investigations, it is very likely that the detective will work with the district attorney's office to obtain search and arrest warrants. It also is likely that in a violent crime investigation, the detective will locate the perpetrator's whereabouts and have to assemble a team of detectives, and Emergency Service Unit (ESU) or SWAT team personnel to apprehend the perpetrator. As you can imagine, you will remove your gun from its holster in many of these scenarios. In fact, I have been involved in arrest and search warrants where the suspect was hiding in the hollowed-out bottom of a platform bed, in the shower, in a closet, and even in a brick chimney. Imagine being surprised by finding such a suspect in any of these situations. Is he armed? Will he have the "drop" on you and already have his weapon aimed and drawn when he is found?

I mentioned the last sector that I am going to discuss in the previous paragraph, the support services units. The support units include ESUs or SWAT, Aviation, Harbor patrol, the Hostage Negotiation Team (HNT), the K-9 unit, the Crime Scene Unit, Computer Crimes, etc. These units become involved and respond when either uniformed patrol or detectives need their assistance. Depending on their specific function, some of these units will not need to remove their weapons from their holsters, while others will have to take out their weapons very often. But remember, they are all still the police, so anything always is possible.

Among these units, members of the ESU or SWAT are the most likely to have to draw their weapons. In the NYPD, it is the ESU team that enters an apartment or location first to apprehend an armed and dangerous, known perpetrator once he/she is located. The NYPD ESU team is equivalent to the SWAT teams in other police departments. ESU and SWAT are the guys who wear the heavy vests and helmets, carry the automatic weapons, and use the cool toys, like the battering rams and tanks. These guys and gals see action constantly.

The other support units typically provide services and do not become involved in dangerous situations, but remember, they still are the police, and anything can happen. In many states, detectives collect evidence and process the crime scene themselves, but in the NYPD, the crime scene unit is called in to collect evidence, dust for prints, and the like. The Hostage Negotiation Team (HNT) is called in to negotiate with hostage takers, barricaded individuals, or individuals threatening suicide. There is a possibility that HNT members will have to remove their weapon from the holster.

Units like Aviation, Harbor, K-9, and Computer Crimes respond to assist patrol officers and detectives when needed. Aviation may assist in a search from the air, while Harbor may locate a person or search for a discarded weapon in a body of water. K-9 may be called in to search for a missing person's scent or help apprehend a perpetrator, and Computer Crimes may be called to a scene when sensitive computer evidence needs to be removed from a crime scene or when a computer needs to be examined in the furtherance of an investigation.

There are other factors that come into play concerning whether an officer has to unholster or use his/her weapon as well. Some say it's based on the officer's luck. I know several officers who have been in multiple shootings on and off duty throughout their careers. Other officers usually say that they have a black cloud over them. I recall a fall evening early in my career. It had to be 1994; I was in the Transit Police Department, assigned to the City-wide Tactical Patrol Force where we rode trains, single-man patrol, in uniform, from point to point (the first stop of the train line to the last stop on the train line) throughout the city.

I was riding a train that was below street-level, but not underground. Passengers entered the station at street-level and then proceeded down the stairs to the platform, which was below street-level but open to the sky. Before being in the Transit Police Department, I had never seen a subway station like this. I had made a few point-to-point runs already and promised myself I'd get off there on my next break to look at how this station was built and how the neighborhood around it looked. I did everything that was required: notified the radio dispatcher that I was detraining and proceeded to the street level to call my command to make the hourly telephone notifications (called hourly rings; made for safety and officer accountability, handheld cell phones were not popular at this time).

After making my rings, I decided to go outside of the subway station to look around. The station was in a seemingly quiet residential neighborhood, across the street from a five or six story housing development. I walked about ten feet along the grass-lined sidewalk, where automobiles were parked along the curb. Suddenly, almost instantaneously, I heard a loud explosion and what sounded like pellets hit the ground at my feet. Based on the sound and the direction of the pellets, I immediately knew I was shot at by someone with a shotgun using buckshot ammunition, from the roof or one of the upper floors of the building across the street.

I immediately took cover behind the parked cars, pulled out my service weapon, and pointed to the multitude of windows and the roof of the building. As I scanned the building and windows, I notified the radio dispatcher that shots were fired and I was shot at. After confirming with the dispatcher that I was not hurt or injured, I requested back-up, and ESU to search the building. The response was tremendous, and the searches were done of the building and the roof, however, nothing was found.

At that point, I remembered what we were often told in roll-call: "Do not get off your train and walk around these neighborhoods. Because we are the Transit Police Department and cover multiple precincts, you do not know what may have happened there last night, or in the past, you have no idea what the climate is on the street." I asked one of the ESU guys if they had found anything. He informed me that it was probably some kid who had just bought or was buying a shotgun and wanted to try it out. He added that their first intention was probably to shoot the weapon into the air, but then he saw you and decided to either have some fun or attempt to kill you. He reiterated that the area is hot and there are gunshots heard every night, all night. I could not believe I had done something so innocent and careless at the same time. I realized that an officer could be doing nothing but wearing the uniform, and danger can come to you. It reminded me that when working, to never take anything lightly and to always be on point. This incident woke me up; it was one of the first events that helped me to realize that policing was real!

The dangers of policing are even greater today. In today's climate, police officers are being ambushed while sitting in their patrol cars. These are terrible situations, but they are a reality. Officers today have to be cognizant of everything going on around them. I use the term "Watch yours and your partner's six!" or "Keep your head on a swivel." Both of these statements became popular because they were used by the military in combat situations. It reminds individuals to watch what's going on behind them and always to look around for danger.

Additional dangers and risk stems from the terrorist climate our country suffers now. Emergency responders run into danger and mishap while the public runs away. That is how it is, and how it is supposed to be. Many lives are lost during terrorist attacks in our country, and many of those are emergency responders. As the possibility of terrorism on United States soil increases, so do the dangers associated with being a police officer, firefighter, and any other emergency responders.

The issues identified here are further evidence that an officer must be on-point, especially when working, and even more importantly, when in uniform.

Chapter 8

Responsibility

Responsibility is an area that some do not realize exists in policing. One of the first responsibilities given to officers is their weapon. The weapon is a huge responsibility that officers will have throughout their careers. It is the officers' responsibility to safeguard their weapons, whether on or off duty, and regardless of where they are. The weapon has to be safeguarded when it is carried and especially when it is not.

Regardless of the type of weapon or the number of weapons you have, you are responsible for all of them. A weapon represents the ability to take a life. This must be taken seriously. The officer has to always consider the worst case scenario. The situation where that weapon gets into the wrong hands and someone gets hurt is the scenario you must think of.

When carrying your weapon off duty, ensure that it is concealed, not because you might scare people and have them call the police to report a person with a gun, but for your own safety. If you're at a location and criminals come in to commit a crime and see your weapon, maybe even before you see them, they have you. They can take you out before you even realize what is happening. What is worse is not only will they have their weapons, but now they will have yours. Of course, seeing your weapon could cause them to cancel their plan and leave, but you have to think and prepare for the worst-case scenario. By having your weapon exposed you are giving up your advantage, the element of surprise, your ability to evaluate and assess the situation. You want the edge in a situation like this.

The other concern is safeguarding your weapon when it is not in your possession. There have been many instances in which children and even adults get hold of a gun and hurt themselves or others. When you store your weapon, it should be in a locked gun box or safe. It is your responsibility to safeguard your weapon when you are off duty. It is your responsibility to make sure it does not end up in the wrong hands. You are responsible for your weapon, and you will be held responsible if something should happen.

When on-duty, it is more obvious that you have to safeguard your weapon. The academy will teach you how to stand, how to blade your body, and to position the weapon away from the suspect. This will become second nature in time. Many officers also keep their hand or arm on their weapon when in uniform. Not gripping the handle or anything like that, just resting their hand, forearm, or elbow on the back of the handle or butt of the gun. This allows the officer to be conscious and aware of the weapon and to provide the advantage of already having contact with the weapon should the need to protect it arise. It may appear to the public that the officer is aggressive; however, it is simply a safeguard. In the 90s in New York, criminals were removing the guns from officer's holsters, and it became more important for officers to safeguard their weapons at all times when in uniform.

Whether working in uniform or plainclothes and in a confrontation, protect your weapon. Whether that confrontation is physical or verbal, protect your weapon. If the confrontation turns physical and you end up rolling around on the ground, protect your weapon. If you end up in a physical confrontation with several perpetrators, protect your weapon. You will learn tactics for protecting your weapon in the academy. If you lose possession of your weapon, not only are you unlikely to survive the confrontation, but your weapon probably will be used to hurt others. Think about it. What kind of person would even try to take a cop's gun? This person is bad. He is going to do bad things when he gets that gun, you cannot let this happen, you must do everything you possibly can to make sure it doesn't happen.

Other responsibilities are related to your duties as a law enforcement professional. Law enforcement is a serious career choice with a high level of responsibility to ensure that everything is done correctly. What I am referring to are the laws, policies, and procedures that you, as an officer are charged to follow. As a law enforcement professional, almost every interaction with the public has a related procedure, and if not followed to the letter, there may be repercussions, including a lawsuit, civilian complaint, reassignment, department charges, and even arrest.

The responsibility is a great one. There are few occupations where you can go to work and while doing your job, end up in trouble. The sad part is, whether or not you've done something wrong, the complaint can be made and will be entertained and investigated. In fact, in most instances, the law enforcement agency you are working for has the responsibility to put the officer on ice until the claims are investigated. On ice could mean suspension or a modified assignment. That may not always be the case, but it does happen often. Be aware of this and when possible, think before you act.

Another huge responsibility is related to criminal procedures. Most do not realize how important this is. As an officer, when something happens, and you respond to the scene, everything matters. Everything, meaning how you learned of the incident, the time you learned of it, how you responded - streets traveled, emergency lights on/off, the route taken, the time of arrival, and every single thing that happened once you arrived. The details of every single job, radio run, and 911 call have the potential to end up in court where your actions can either be scrutinized or can be the main factor that determines whether a defendant is convicted or released. As the detective assigned to and responsible for a case, your actions are even more important. You will conduct interviews, interrogations and line-ups, collect evidence, execute search and arrest warrants, and make arrests. Each of these steps have associated laws and procedures that are a mile long, and every detail must be followed exactly.

This particular area of responsibility is important because if you forget an important step like reading the suspect his rights, conduct a line-up incorrectly, collect evidence incorrectly, or make a mistake in another important area, an entire case could suffer. A guilty individual could be set free, or an individual or family could lose their opportunity to receive the closure and satisfaction they deserve and need. This not only would cause you issues with the agency for which you work for and the District Attorney's office handling the case, but you have to live with it. You will have to live with the fact that your error weakened or destroyed a case to the extent that the suspect may have been released or prosecution denied.

As a Detective, this would be tough because you have probably become relatively close to the victim and the family. You may have reassured them numerous times that the perpetrator will be apprehended and the case will lead to a conviction. They have put their hopes and trust in you and the investigation you were conducting. The victim and the family have come to every court proceeding to watch and learn the details of the case. They are very involved and are expecting a good, well-executed case. You would bear the guilt of letting them down.

The other issue would come from the District Attorney's Office. Law enforcement and the District Attorney's Office are supposed to work together to combat crime and prosecute offenders. Police officers are expected to be trained and experienced in following the laws and procedures related to the apprehension of criminals. Detectives are held to a slightly higher standard than officers on patrol because in addition to having a clear understanding of arrest procedures, detectives are expected to understand the practices and procedures with respect to investigations, witnesses, evidence, and even the law. There are many instances in which patrol will make an arrest and contact the Detective squad to find out what they have, what specific crime and level of crime to charge. Therefore, when you are working with the District Attorney's office, they expect that everything was done correctly and according to the established laws and procedures. An error could be an embarrassment to the officer, the detective, the precinct or detective unit where the member works, and the agency associated. The word that the evidence was mishandled, or a line-up, show-up, witness testimony, or suspect interrogation damaged a case, would spread like wildfire, and could tarnish your entire career.

Chapter 9

Advice for Law Enforcement

T his chapter provides insight for those seriously considering a law enforcement career and reinforcement for those currently a member of law enforcement. Whether you are planning to take the exam, have already passed the exam and are in the hiring process, or are a new officer, the information in this chapter, which is related to finance, safety, and to survive the difficult issues and times, is paramount. Although your academy training will teach you about or touch upon some of the issues discussed here briefly, much of the information comes from several sources encompassing years of experience. The information in this chapter derives from years of advice given to me, talking "smack" in the locker room with the guys, and insight gained from thinking things through and replaying scenarios. The advice here is in no way complete and all-encompassing. It is just a small sample of some of the information law enforcement professionals need to be cognizant of.

The first three pieces of advice are related and pertain to the wellbeing of the law enforcement professional overall. The first and most important piece of advice for someone pursuing any law enforcement career that involves even the slightest possibility of danger is:

Make sure you go home at the end of your shift. There is nothing more important than making sure that whatever you get into during your shift, whether on the street or behind a desk, whether in uniform or plainclothes, regardless of rank, you are alive and able to go home at the end of the day. Your safety is paramount. Yes, we are committed and dedicated to saving others' lives, and often take risks and find ourselves in situations others would not consider, but at the end of the day, we all want to go home to our loved ones and families in one piece.

The second important thing to remember is:

CYA: Cover Your Ass

This can be interpreted in many ways and can mean different things to different people and in different situations. The obvious meaning is to be cognizant of everything around you and ensure that you are not caught off guard. This also relates to your partner. You and your partner have an obligation when working together never to allow anything bad to happen to each other. Therefore, common sayings are "Keep your head on a swivel" and "Watch your six" which means to keep looking around and behind you constantly, watching everything that is going on, so you don't get caught off guard. Because none of us have eyes in the backs of our heads, it is important that our partners watch our backs. What we can't see, our partners should see, and the converse.

CYA is related closely to the third piece of advice I have, which my instructors in the Police Academy stressed:

Articulate, Articulate, Articulate!

To articulate means to explain or express something coherently and clearly. This goes hand in hand with CYA, because in some instances, to cover your ass, you will have to talk your way clear. What it comes down to is being prepared to have a good explanation for everything that you do. This holds true when a boss or supervisor questions your actions or lack thereof. For example, you and your partner get a radio call that is eight blocks away. It takes you 20 minutes to get there. When you arrive, your supervisor is there already, asking you why it took you so long to arrive, and explains further that he came from 30 blocks away and arrived there before you. Have an explanation ready, a good one. There probably will be a good explanation for your late arrival, but if not, come up with one before you get there. Either way, confer with your partner, be on the same page with your answers, and be ready to give your response calmly and not as if you're upset because someone is asking.

Articulation also is important when in the field, in court, or when speaking with the Assistant District Attorney about what you did concerning a case or police incident. If you have put handcuffs on the victim of a crime and have him/her sitting on the sidewalk, be ready to explain why to the supervisor who arrives on the scene, the Assistant District Attorney in her office, and in court if it should come up. I was always taught to think things through and be able to explain the circumstances and reasons why I did or did not do something when asked. If you are not asked, do not volunteer information. It may be obvious why you did or did not do something, and you may not be asked. Consequently, don't be the bumbling fool at the scene or in court explaining something that was not asked, as it could make you appear incompetent.

Articulation can also allow you to talk your way out of situations with the public and perpetrators. Learn to think quickly and be able to explain clearly why things have, or must occur. Do not simply have the attitude: because I'm the police and I said so. Although that is needed at times, there are times when that attitude will make situations worse.

An important piece of advice that was touched on briefly in the previous chapter that can keep you out of trouble with your department, the courts, and the public is to learn your craft. As much as possible, learn every aspect of the specific assignment or job you are doing. Law enforcement is different from most professions. An error on your part could have enormous repercussions for you, your agency, and everyone involved. Lawsuits, criminal cases being dismissed, and disciplinary action are all at stake. Therefore, you must learn your craft and know what you are doing out there. That includes knowing the laws, policies, procedures, and tactics involved with your assignment. If you do car stops, learn every aspect of car stops, including the legal aspect, tactics, and your agency's policies and procedures. If you are assigned to a unit that executes search warrants regularly, learn the laws, policies, procedures, and tactics involved with search warrants.

Learning your craft is also important because your supervisors, who are supposed to direct and guide you, may not know the important aspects of the assignment. They may not be giving you needed information or may be giving you flawed information. You need to be able to recognize this. Although the supervisor giving you the order or assignment is ultimately responsible, you also hold some responsibility as well and could bear the brunt of it.

Another piece of advice that I feel is important to mention early, right after your all around wellbeing, is a money issue. Many retirees will tell you that the job is fun, exciting, and thrilling; others will say it sucks, drains and uses you, and is relentless. However, whether they loved or hated the job, the one thing which most retirees would agree on is to get your money right. Most would concur that you should start planning your retirement from the day you start the job. That means to take advantage of every savings vehicle available. As I mentioned in Chapter one, there are numerous financial retirement benefits in most law enforcement agencies. In fact, most have all the same retirement vehicles as does private industry, plus the pension. At retirement, in addition to the pension and eventually social security, there are other options available to save money towards retirement. One of the first that most mention is the Deferred Compensation Plan. Deferred Compensation is an investment/saving plan that allows employees to save additional income towards retirement through payroll deduction. The plan consists of a 457 and a 401(k) plan, both of which offer pre-tax and after-tax options (nyc.gov/deferredcomp). If you join Deferred Compensation at the beginning of your career, it is very likely that you will accrue $500,000 to 1 million dollars in this account. This may sound extreme, but it isn't, I have seen it happen over and over again.

Another option that will allow you to have more money at retirement is the Increased Take Home Pay (ITHP) waiver. With ITHP you elect to contribute an additional 5% of your pay towards your pension. There is also the 50% additional contributions option, which when you initiate it, adds 50% of the pension contribution required to the current contribution rate (nyc.gov/nycppf). Both of these options allow the law enforcement professional to have a larger pension at retirement.

So, as you can see, police departments have retirement benefits similar to those in the private sector, plus the pension, so take advantage wherever you can. It should be noted that the ITHP and 50% increased contributions are not available through all law enforcement agencies and are also being challenged in some areas; therefore, depending on its status in your agency or area, it may not be available.

For stability, promotional opportunities within the police department, and to be able to have a future outside and after the job, I suggest that you pursue further education. One of the things I liked about being in law enforcement is the way they encourage you to continue your education. As I said in Chapter one, most police departments have scholarships available for those who want to continue their education. The NYPD has its own scholarship unit with over 60 scholarships available for its officers. These scholarships are for law enforcement and should be available through individual departments around the country. Additionally, the schools in the states, towns, and areas specific to each department may have their own scholarships for their local law enforcement as well. Many of these are financial, but some offer paid leave in the form of several days to several months of paid time off to study and complete assignments. As I also mentioned in

Chapter one, I earned my Masters degree through an NYPD Educational Leave Scholarship. It opened the door for me to continue beyond the undergraduate level and to realize more options for my future, after the job.

Other options exist through promotional exams within the department you choose. Each department has a patrol guide or similar guide that provides the rules and procedures specific to that department. It is an extensive guide that covers everything possible, from how to wear your uniform to responding to terrorist attacks. Those who wish to pursue the ranks of Sergeant, Lieutenant, and Captain, must study this guide and know its details like the back of their hands. By passing these promotional exams, you will have the ability to earn more money, take on greater responsibility, and prepare for a supervisory or management position when you retire, if you choose. Many feel that "making rank" is the only way to go. If this is, or becomes your thought, don't hesitate, study, and do it!

On the safety side, there are several issues that need to be stated. First and most important, always wear your bullet-proof vest, regardless of whether you are working inside or outside the stationhouse. A bullet-proof vest is a tool to help ensure that you will go home to your family even if the worst-case scenario becomes a reality. In that scenario there is one chance to get it right; make sure you have given yourself that chance.

Another safety suggestion is always to know where you are. There are many instances in which an officer and his partner are moving around, whether in a police car or on foot. If an emergency involving you or your partner occurs, such as shots fired at you, you will have to call for backup and give your location. If you don't know your location, you can't give it to the radio dispatcher, and units responding will have a difficult time finding you. You don't want to be in that position. While walking on foot patrol, either in uniform or plainclothes, look around and keep track of the street you are on and the cross streets in the area. The same applies when patrolling in the police car. Make this a habit and make sure to discuss it with your partner so that he/she is doing the same. If you work in a specific location all the time, you will learn the area ultimately, but in the beginning, it will require a conscious effort.

A suggestion that played a big role during my patrol days while with the New York City Transit Police Department was always to keep my back to the wall. Before 1995, New York City had three separate police departments, the NYPD, the New York City Transit Police Department, and the New York City Housing Police Department. Each department had its own training academy that tailored the training to the specifics of each assignment. In the Transit Police Department, patrols were single-man, and some assignments were citywide. Single-man patrols in areas where we were unfamiliar was a dangerous combination, but it's what I signed up for, so it's what I did. During this time, as I mentioned earlier in the previous chapter, police officer's weapons were being taken. The Transit Police Department had just switched from the .38 caliber revolver to the Glock 9mm semi-automatic pistol, and the bad guys wanted them. There were several reports of Transit Police officers having their weapons taken because they were patrolling alone. When patrolling on foot, especially when working without a partner, it becomes imperative to cover and protect yourself any

133

way you can. It is impossible to see behind you and therefore it is imperative that you cut down the size of the area you need to be aware of. Keeping your back to the wall reduces the threat area considerably. With your back to the wall you are able to focus on the front, left, and right, and eliminate the possibility of a threat from the rear. This is a tactic I learned in the New York City Transit Police Academy, in addition to keeping my arm or elbow on my weapon, in its holster, when in public. These two tactics are essential during single-man patrol.

Additional advice would be that if you find yourself in or entering a situation where gunplay may take place, take cover. Position yourself behind an object that will help shield you from the gunfire. Examples of cover are a wall, a car, being behind a corner, a large dumpster, etc. If you are facing gunfire and do not have cover, you are likely to return fire immediately. The theory is that if you have cover, you will have time to assess the situation before firing your weapon arbitrarily. Now, I do understand that this is a theory, and it may be difficult to think this way when you're in a foot pursuit with an armed assailant, and he turns the corner ahead of you. However, considering your safety, I hope you will be able to think this way and stop at the corner to peek around before rounding it. By practicing these possible scenarios, you may be able to train yourself to act and react in a certain way reflexively. Muscle memory is a powerful ally.

The other advice that gave me a sense of security was to always carry a reliable backup weapon. On patrol, I carried the Glock 9mm service weapon, a .38 caliber detective special backup weapon in my waistband or in a shoulder holster under my jacket, as well as a large folding knife. If there were ever a problem with my semi-automatic 9mm, the .38 revolver was my back-up, and if all else failed I had the knife for close combat situations. After becoming a detective, my weapons of choice changed. In certain situations, I'd carry the Glock 9mm service weapon, a second smaller Glock 9mm as the backup weapon, and the knife. Looking back, that was a lot of firepower, but it was New York City, and I may have needed it.

Another good reason to carry a backup weapon is should you find yourself in a situation where you have to approach someone and appear unarmed. They would see the Glock 9mm in your holster as you approached; while they wouldn't see the backup weapon, held behind your back or turned away from the suspect with your hand slightly behind your leg as you approached them. In the world in which we live today, an officer can never have too many assurances. Better safe than sorry. The saying goes: Better to be judged by 12 than to be carried by 6.

The next piece of advice is a simple one. It involves your behavior when dealing with the public. First, treat everyone with respect until they give you cause to do otherwise. Regardless of their station in life, regardless of whether they are a homeless person, a victim, a witness, or a perpetrator, everyone deserves your respect. Keep in mind that you should treat everyone the way that you would want another officer to treat your family or loved ones. By maintaining this thought process, you will maintain your composure and your professionalism. You'd be surprised how kindness can make a person calm down and come to their senses. In my experience they will see what you are doing and appreciate it. It doesn't always work out this way, as there are times when the person you are dealing with is becoming physical or creating a dangerous situation and you have to become stern or put your hands on them. Try to make this your last resort, without putting yourself or others in unnecessary danger. This approach has worked for me numerous times, especially in hostile and emotional hostage negotiation situations. As I mentioned earlier in the book, don't let them hook your child. Maintain your composure; you are the professional.

To piggy-back off the previous piece of advice about treating everyone with respect until they give you a reason to do otherwise, you should remember that there is video everywhere to keep you honest. We live in the technology era, and everyone has video cameras, cell phones, etc. Further, there are surveillance cameras everywhere, not to mention the body-camera you may be wearing or the dashboard camera mounted in your police vehicle. We live in a time where the media covers and pays well for compromising video. Be cognizant of what you are doing and saying. A video in court is often considered solid evidence that can be difficult to dispute.

137

As you build your law enforcement career, my advice for those who have, or are considering having a family, is to always make time for your loved ones. They can be the strength and serenity that allow you to get through the tough days and weeks you face on the job. Your spouse or partner can provide stability through many uncertain times. He/she will be one of the reasons you push and continue on the tough path that life often creates. Take your days off and spend time with family to help relieve stress and refocus on the normality of life and the importance of what you have outside the job.

I'd also add: separate the job from your life and do not bring your work home. Leave all conflict and strife at the door and welcome the love and innocence that your family can provide. There is nothing better than having a rough day and coming home to your children running to you as you walk in and your partner meeting you at the door with love and affection. This is very important. Establish this, communicate this, and if you're lucky, you can have this.

Another piece of advice I'd like to give is for everyone entering law enforcement. The advice is to stay

138

in shape and train in self-defense, boxing, or martial arts. Being in shape and having the confidence that accompanies the skills you've learned can be important when dealing with people. In law enforcement, there can be foot chases, physical altercations, and times when you have to use force to put someone on a wall or secure them. Your physical condition and abilities become important in these instances. In fact, it could be the difference between getting hurt or even killed.

It is also important to stay in shape because law enforcement is a tough, stressful career choice that often takes a toll on your body and mind. The best way to combat these pressures is to stay active, fit, and healthy. All departments have gyms or fitness centers for their officers; use them. Health care is provided one way or another, use that as well. Mental health care is available within the department and through your health care provider, and you should seek and use it when necessary. The objective is to complete your career and be healthy, wealthy, and strong enough to retire and start a second career or live the retired life that you should have been planning from day one.

Finally, you will hear a lot of negative talk about being in law enforcement; the salary, lack of respect, danger, and racial issues. Do not listen. Like everything in life, a career in law enforcement has its ups and downs. However, if this is what you want, if it's your calling, pay no attention to the masses. Just do it! Go in with a positive attitude, understanding that there will be difficulties; things will not always be as you want or think they should be. Accept the things you cannot change and change what you can change. Most of all, have fun, enjoy the experience and opportunity, and survive to live a long life on the pension you've earned. As I and many of my law enforcement brothers and sisters say:

Enjoy the ride… it's the greatest show on earth!

About the Author

The author of this book, Dr. Alfred S. Titus, Jr., grew up in Jamaica, Queens, New York. Alfred attended Aviation High School in his early pursuit of becoming an airline pilot. After high school, he obtained his bachelor's degree in Electro-Mechanical Computer Technology in his new pursuit to be part of the technology revolution. After working in the computer field for several years, he decided to pursue his life-long dream of being a law enforcement agent. He joined the New York City Police Department with the intention of making a difference and touching lives.

Officer Titus began by working in the subways in Harlem and Washington Heights, New York, where he learned the community and the job first hand. He was an active and dedicated police officer who moved quickly into plainclothes assignments. His diligence provided him the opportunity to work with the Manhattan Robbery Squad where he earned the rank of Detective. He transferred later to the Manhattan Night-Watch Squad where his attention to detail on several high-profile cases gained the attention of the Manhattan South Homicide Squad. Within a year, Detective Titus became a member of the Manhattan South Homicide Squad, a prestigious unit within NYPD's Detective Bureau. During his 11 years in the Homicide Squad, he led numerous high-profile cases that ended in arrest and conviction. His success in Homicide earned him two promotions within the Detective rank, allowing him to reach the top rank of Detective First Grade. While in Homicide, he became a member of the NYPD's elite Hostage Negotiation Team (HNT) and was trained as a Negotiator. As a Hostage Negotiator, he helped save the lives of several emotionally disturbed persons and bring an end to several crisis situations.

In addition to his career, while working in the NYPD, Detective Titus earned his master's degree through a Police Department scholarship and taught a two-day Homicide course for the NYPD Citizen Police Academy. He also began work as a part-time Adjunct Lecturer at John Jay College of Criminal Justice while working toward his Ph.D. in Public Policy and Administration with a specialization in Criminal Justice, all the while juggling the demanding schedule and workload of the Homicide Squad. He retired from the NYPD in July 2016 to complete his doctorate and pursue a second career as an educator and consultant. He completed his doctoral dissertation on Community Policing and earned his Ph.D. in 2017.

The Personal Side of Policing is his second book. The first, Forward Motion... the Keys to Progress and Success! is a motivational tool for all ages. The book provides insight into achieving your dreams and goals, staying away from the pitfalls of life, and removing barriers. The book was rated #1 in its category for the first three weeks of publication on Amazon. The book is available in Kindle and paperback form through the following link:

http://www.amazon.com/dp/B078RCB56J.

Dr. Titus has created a consulting firm, A. Titus Consulting, LLC, to pursue goals that include creating additional literature that addresses issues in law enforcement, research related to criminal justice, educating our youth, and all things related to social change and empowerment. He continues to teach at John Jay College of Criminal Justice, where he is an Assistant Professor, and at Grand Canyon University through their online Criminal Justice Program. He also volunteers with the Thurgood Marshall Mock Trial Program, where he mentors 7th and 8th graders on topics related to the law, the legal process, and courtroom procedures in preparation for an annual courtroom/trial competition.

Dr. Titus' earlier articles and works are listed below:

Ph.D. Dissertation:

- *Realigning Community Policing in a Homeland Security Era*
  http://scholarworks.waldenu.edu/dissertations/4106/

- *Who is Looking Out for Us... the Lowering of Police Hiring Standards.*
  http://linkedin.com/pulse/who-looking-out-us-lowering-police-hiring-standards-alfred-titus-mpa

- *Transparency in Policing*
  https://jpublicpolicy.com/2016/03/05/transparency-in-policing-through-nypds-citizens-police-academy/

Dr. Titus can be contacted for panel discussions, speaking engagements, and media consulting at:

A. Titus Consulting, LLC

P.O. Box 1056

Valley Stream, NY 11582

Email: ATitus@ATitusConsulting.com

Website: www.ATitusConsulting.com

References:

Greenhut, S. (2014). Police and fire continue to promote
'early death' fiction. Public Sector, Inc.
Pensions, Public Safety Unions. Retrieved from
http://www.publicsectorinc.org/2014/08/police-
and-fire-continue-to-promote-their-early-death-
untruth/

NYC PBA Health & Welfare Benefits Bulletin (2013).
Annuity. Volume 1, Number 1. Retrieved from
https://www.nycpba.org/benefits/newsletter-
1306.pdf

NYPD Recruit.com (2018)– New York's Finest Salary
& Benefits information – Retrieved from
http://www1.nyc.gov/site/nypd/careers/careers.pa
ge

NYPD Scholarship Unit (2015) – Retrieved from
https://www1.nyc.gov/html/nypd/downloads/pdf/
training_bureau/2015_scholarship_guide.pdf

State of New York Insurance Department (2009). Report
on Examination of the New York City Police
Officers' Variable Supplements Fund as of June
30, 2004. Retrieved from
http://www.dfs.ny.gov/insurance/exam_rpt/n567
8c04.pdf